What the Sam Hill

FORT MADISON.

I Never Left the Room.

(What the Sam Hill.)

WHAT THE SAM HILL

BY
WIB. F. CLEMENTS

BROADWAY PUBLISHING CO.
835 Broadway, New York

BRANCH OFFICES: CHICAGO, WASHINGTON, BALTIMORE,
ATLANTA, NORFOLK, FLORENCE, ALA.

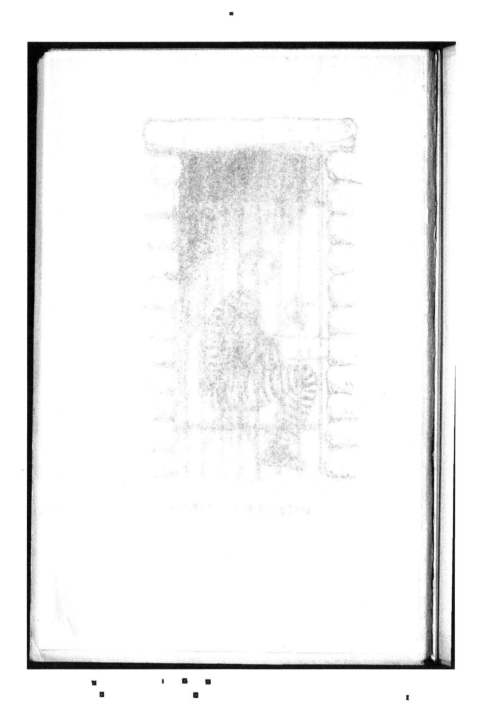

WHAT THE SAM HILL

BY
WIB. F. CLEMENTS

BROADWAY PUBLISHING CO.
835 Broadway, New York
BRANCH OFFICES: CHICAGO, WASHINGTON, BALTIMORE,
ATLANTA, NORFOLK, FLORENCE. ALA.

1911

PREFACE.

To my old friends Callister, Enyart and Bishop, I dedicate this book. May it help to while away an hour. In the fight between Puff and the Jew we sometimes wonder what would have happened to Puff had he actually got hurt. We make no pretentions to authorship. Many of the things mentioned happened in actual life. We launch the little boat. Hoist the sail and bid it Bon voyage.   Wib.

WHAT THE SAM HILL

CHAPTER I

Write a book? And why not. It always been my desire to write a book. When I was a boy in school I (and that was not last week) used to write short sketches, biographies of my schoolmates, picturing them as men of sixty and having lived a useful life, and all that.

What, you write a book? You, over sixty years old.

Yes, why not? All I lack is a name.

Well, I'll swan; what the sam hill!

There ye are. The very thing. That shall be the name—What the Sam Hill. Now you are foolin'. No, I am not. I am going to call it "What the Sam Hill."

I might begin by saying that I am a son of poor but honest parents, who would have died childless if there had not been five of us children. But I won't say anything of the kind. I merely say I am here and pretty well tickled that such is the case. In fact, ever since I have known anything I have never felt like I wanted to trade this world for any other one; however, when they get the wireless telegraphy going and we hear from some of the other places I may change my mind.

I have always been of a roving disposition, which may account for the fact that I have never gathered much moss. Now, I don't expect this book to have as many words in it as the one Noah Webster wrote, and I hardly think the spelling will be as good. If you should run across a word now and then you don't understand, just turn to Noah Webster's latest book, and if you don't find the meaning why, I'll lose faith in Noah, and I'd hate to do that, for Noah has always been a particular friend of mine, and I owe largely my knowledge and smartness to my close friendship with him.

Noah was always more for explaining things than I was; in fact, you will notice all through his book he stops to explain the meaning of his words, until you almost lose sight of the hero, the story; and the minor characters you have lost sight of altogether. The Mr. Johnson of the story you can partly follow, but end men and those sitting along between you lose sight of.

I've little doubt, however that Noah's book will outlast mine; I believe, though, that if Noah had not been called hence he would have been willing to have divided honors even

[6]

with me: There wasn't anything small about Noah.

In some of my short sketches I spoke of, I once got a letter from an old schoolmate who had got one of them; he wrote me it took him back to our old boyhood days. He shed tears over some of the things mentioned (especially where I had taken a licking for some of his tricks and wouldn't blow on him), and laughed at some of the droll ones. Said he had never left his room from the time he commenced it until finished. This swelled me up some until I afterward learned he was, at the time, working for the State and resided in Ft. Madison. His letter was written before the crime of '73; and must not be confounded as to truthfulness with politicians of later days. He never explained just what particular pull he had in getting a State position, and it has nothing particular to do with this book.

CHAPTER II

In speaking of old boyhood days, the letter brought up an amusing incident in which his interest was about equal to mine. We usually did our swimming in Duck Creek, where, if any one made an extra hazardous dive, the greater part of his back was still out of water, but on this occasion or trip we went down on Wolf creek to swim, where the water was twenty-two inches deep by actual measurement. The swimming, however, was of small moment. It was after coming out and putting on our shirts wrong side out (which caused no end of abbreviation to explain away after getting home), we started home across the creek bottom, and, as blind luck would have it, ran spang into Will Fletcher's watermelon patch. Here now our Sunday School training bore down very hard, but by a kind of compromise between conscience and hunger we cut one open. We had figured a little like they do out in Leadville that possession was nine points, and we would chance it on the other point. We had gotten into the heart of the subject when I heard something whack together and on looking up saw it was my companion's knees. A far-away look of "meet

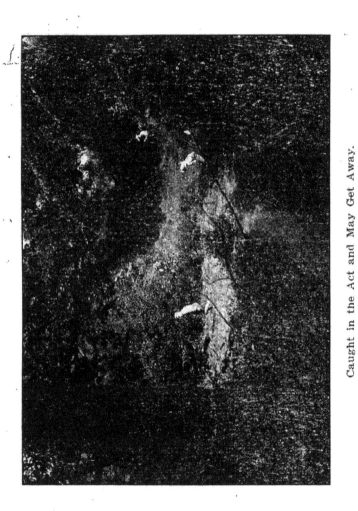

Caught in the Act and May Get Away.

(What the Sam Hill.)

me when the moon goes down" was on his
face; his hat had raised until it merely touched
the bumps of cowardice and secretiveness, and
his finger—not unlike a skeleton hand—was
pointing to a man just stepping out from behind a tree.

Now, my companion was somewhat acquainted with some of the peculiarities of
Will, but I was not loaded down with such
knowledge, and, furthermore, had never been
intimate with him, so did not stay to get better acquainted, but went up the hollow
through the timber. Even my new Barlow
was left sticking bolt upright in the red bosom
of our victim, to appear at a later date as evidence against me, as I, in an unguarded moment, had carved my name: "W. I. B." on
the handle—a practice I have always looked
down on ever since. My companion, seeing
that I was in a fair way to escape, put a bold
face on the matter, and by the time Will
reached him had got his knees working, but
the squirrel rifle carried by Will made him
think it not a bad idea to make friends with
him, which he did by placing all the blame on
me, and his story, along with the Barlow,
made a clean case against me.

I have never felt like falling on his neck
since, and learning where he was employed
when he wrote me about the story—the old
story has ever rung in my ears: "The mills of
the gods grind slowly, but exceedingly fine."

[9]

In mentioning boyhood days, so many things come back to us. I suppose my school days were about the same as other boys. I started in what was called the "old brick," about one-half mile from town. Boys came from quite a distance—it seemed quite a distance—but in after years, after roaming over a country where no trees were in sight, where the prairie dog held full sway, and then looking back at the country surrounding the "old brick," I now know none of them came very far. In after years I was transferred to Pin Hook school up on the pike, and finally to the New Castle Seminary. Here our boyhood pranks began to be curtailed. One eye-sore to us was the study hour at night. The principal, Rice by name, issued orders that no scholar should be on the street after seven o'clock in the evening without written permission. This was hard on the average boy. It made playing after night hazardous, but added enticement to it from the fact that it was forbidden. The principal was a very tall man, and fleet on foot, and was the last man to leave the street at night. It was our business to look out for Rice, as we called him to his back. We would change clothes with boys not in school. We would turn our coats wrong side out, cap with rim behind, and all kinds of disguises, but few of these duped the professor. A man with a guilty conscience is a coward, and few of us could stand and let him

A Test of Endurance.

(*What the Sam Hill.*)

come up to us. We would start in with a good stock of bravado, but when he got close to us we would fail and turn to fly, this invariably ending in our being caught, and punishment in various forms quickly followed.

I well remember in my own case I was the champion runner of our set and tried one night to match my speed with the professor. I had a hundred feet the start, but do the best I could I could not widen the breach. It was across streets, down alleys, through buildings, and everywhere I glanced back showed the old man holding his own.

The bystanders shouted, "Git there!" "You'll make it!" "Hoe it down!" It soon became a certainty I was a gonner, but, by a superhuman effort, I rounded a corner a little in advance and turned down an alley where there was a lot of lumber piled upon some large timbers. It was but the work of a moment to drop flat on the ground and roll under one of these piles. It must have been a minute that I never drew my breath, so quiet did I lay, but the night was chilly and a strong draught under where I lay soon began to tell. I would first listen from this side, then that, but could hear nothing. Then a cold chill would course down my back, but I must stick it out a little longer. He may be there. But I could stand it no longer; it was move or freeze. I moved so slowly and quietly that I made no noise at all. I rolled out from

under the pile, straightened up, when whack!
came his hand down on my shoulder; and so
strong was it that I thought he would pinch a
piece out of it.

"Ah, ah, Philander! I have you now!" (I
had Philander's coat on.) He had made sure
it was Philander.

I says, "I guess not." This staggered him
a moment only, for he struck a match, and by
its flash recognized me.

"You will apologize before the whole school
in the morning, or be expelled."

This I did, and I think to this day my parents never heard of it. I would advise all boys
to make the best of their advantages in school
and not follow in the footsteps of that age,
and I expect the boys to follow the advice as
close as I would have followed it then.

Ahead of the Hounds. Helping the Old Coon Dog Over the Log.

(*What the Sam Hill.*)

CHAPTER III

"Hello, Puff! How are ye?"

"Oh, not first class."

"What's the matter—the old boss found his strap?"

"Yes, that's a part of it. I don't set down now in the presence of my betters."

"Gee, is it as bad as that?"

"Yes, ever since I quit school I——"

"Quit school? I didn't know you had quit."

"Yes, my education is finished."

Day after to-morrow will be two days since I quit."

"Well, say, Puff, I don't like that. Who are we going to soak now in the bull pen? You and Danget and I furnished most of the amusement there."

"I don't care; you will have to get along without me.

I was a little lonesome at first, but now I have got used to it. The school days seem like a dream of long ago."

"I don't care, it's going to be dull. How's old Nice?"

"Oh, he's all right; had him out coon hunting last night—only had to go back twice to help him over a log."

"He must be getting in his second puphood, sure.

I can remember when it took some to go in front and look for coons, and some to follow behind to help Old Nice over the logs."

"Yes, Danget, Jim, Oscar and I were down in Uncle Billy Lynn's sugar camp last night and had a good hunt."

"I understand. I reckon you don't happen to know where old Dr. Cruse's old setting hen is this morning?"

"What's that! Setting hen! Who's talking about setting hens?"

"Well, I made a slight remark myself."

"If the hen is missing, Hugh, I guess I wouldn't have to go far to find the cause. There wasn't any light in Genn's kitchen when I came back past there, and all the old folks gone, leaving Dave to keep house. I believe I'd lay low on the setting hen, anyhow, until old Doc says he's lost one."

"I talked with Dudley this morning. He never said anything about losing a hen. I've known fellows to give themselves away before now."

"You think you're a little smart since you quit school, don't ye? Been reading Old Sleuth, ain't ye? Don't git out'n your latitude, Puff. I've known fellows to refuse to set down in the presence of their betters for worse cause than a boot strap."

"Maybe you think you can do it?"

Sawing Stove Wood Saturday Night by Lantern Light.

(*What the Sam Hill.*)

"If you'll just step down in the alley, I'll show ye."

"Hello, boys! What's the row?"

"How are ye, Dick?"

"Good morning, W. I. B. What's the matter with Puff?"

"Oh, ever since he quit school he's been putting it on a little thick, and I was just inviting him down in the alley back of Kinard Burris' stable to argue the case."

"Oh, well, hold on! Old Kilgore's in town; saw him come this morning, least said soonest mended, boys. I seen him whittling with an old Barlow that had a mighty familiar look. I tried to see the handle, but couldn't make it, but I'd lay low if I was you."

"Lyman, come here. There ain't wood enough to get dinner."

"Listen at that! Doggonned if I aint' a notion to start to school again. A fellow didn't have to cut stove-wood there, anyhow."

"Oh, go and cut your mother some wood; you ought to have cut enough Saturday to last all week."

"How are ye, W. I. B.? I passed your wood house Saturday night as I was going down to Tom Powers' store, and seen you cuttin' wood by a lantern."

"Look here, Puff, I won't wait to take you down to the alley, if you don't watch out."

"Hold on here, boys; I ain't going to have any fighting going on here, I tell ye, while old Kilgore's in town. I was along when old Granny Fletcher's grapes disappeared, and I saw the same old basket with one handle off (that I ran off and left under the tree), right here in our store this morning with a lot of Squire Kilgore's eggs in it, and I tell ye things have got to be kept quiet while he's in town."

"Look here, Puff, what did you quit school for, anyhow?"

"Well, me and old Wess Killen couldn't agree. Now I used to get along with Bill Mc-Whorter, and Rose Miller, and all of them; but we didn't have to write letters and essays with them, but old Wess is a terror. You know I never cared much for grammar, anyhow, and about all I knew about geography was the road from Blooming Grove to old Joe Hay's swimming hole on Duck creek, or old Levi Osborn's peach orchard. I could locate them with one eye shet, and I have been in Bob Wilson's orchard, too; and I wasn't alone, either. You needn't look so skeered, I ain't blowing on any one to-day, Kilgore's in town. As I said before, Killen's a terror. It was essay or a lickin', and as I had had so many lickin's, I thought I would try an essay for a change."

"Yea, W. I. B. and I was there and heard part of that essay, but we was a little startled at the windup of it, and would like to hear the rest of it."

"All right, but I guess I'll have to cut some wood first."

"All right; W. I. B. and I will meet you down in the buggy shed, Dick. I kind o' hate to have Puff quit school."

"So do I. I had got in practice in the bull pen, and could soak him every time. It will be hard on Danget, now."

"Yes, it will; how's the squirrels now?"

"Somebody let them out. Yes, clean gone. Got a cake to sell now. You don't think Lush Doughty had anything to do with it, do you?"

"No, I guess not. All he thinks about now. is the girls."

"What, that little rip?"

"Yes, he's little, but he is three years older than you and me, you know."

"Do ye reckon we will like the girls in three years, Dick?"

"I rather think not."

CHAPTER IV

"Well, fellows, I've got wood enough cut for night and morning, both. I thought while I was at it I'd cut a lot of it. Now, as for the essay, I spent considerable time on it, as I knew old Wess would not have no half-way business. He said it was enough to test a man's religion to have such a fellow around, and as I had seen Uncle Billy breaking out a patch of new ground, the thought struck me that 'A Test of Religion' would be a good subject.

"The test of a man's religion is to place him plowing in a stumpy piece of ground near the church, while quarterly meeting is going on, and give him a black and brindle pair of steers at the plow, who have been restless from birth and dull of comprehension, and an appetite that is 'unquenchable and fadeth not away.' These combination and the proximity of the church, and the nearness of the presiding elder, all holding him back from using language adequate to the occasion. Should he pass from one end of the field to the other with countenance serene, you must say the test is good. He stands eighty-five per cent., and instruct the secretary to so write.

[18]

(*What the Sam Hill.*)　·　A Test of Religion.

"When you say why subject him to all this, when you should know that we are instructed from the start that you shall have time to erase the 'sweat from your brow,' but still labor for what you eat (the resolution of the American Federation of Labor to the contrary, notwithstanding). You see, Dick, I thought it well enough to sling in a few big words (old Wess is great on big words), and his patch of ground, as to stones, resembles a farm in Maine (where you have to buy whiskey by the barrel, and that measured in an old musket barrel), or an abandoned Hoosier farm of blackberry bushes, compared with this of his, sinks out of sight, and the thought goes spinning up his backbone as each brier swings back across his bare ankles (for understand this test was made before wool was placed on the free list, and the price of cosmoline and arnica salve had advanced), and you ask him why these things are, and he tells you, 'to raise corn to winter these pesky steers, so I can plow up this patch next year to raise more corn to winter these steers on,' and you leave him extending and extending and extending until you imagine Gabriel's horn cuts in and stops it all, as no Union Labor or People's Party ever stopped anything, and this relic of former grandeur or promise sinks from sight as thousands have before him, and when Old Wess——"

"That will be enough of that, Lyman; we will excuse you on the remainder of it."

"Now, boys, don't you think he ought to have let me read it all?" .

"Why, yes, Puff; it's good."

"Well, he didn't, and kept me after school, and said he would only give me half a thrashing. He may have called it a half, but I think he forgot himself, and forgot all about the credits I ought to have had. Now this, and a slight misunderstanding between Jake and I has about finished my education."

"It's too blamed bad, Puff, but you'd better come back, anyhow; we all catch it once in a while, you know."

"Yes, I know; but I don't want much education, anyhow. Danget and I have been planning a little trip, and I'd as soon quit now as any time."

"Where ye going?"

"Well, I don't know; Danget has two or three books written by a Mister Beedel, describing some fine country out on the Platt river and along the loop and lavy beds of Nebraska. We think of going there."

"Pshaw, Puff, them books are all lies. Pa says they are nothing but yaller back novels, and not one of them so."

"Well, I don't know. Danget says they are, and I guess he has read about as many of them as any one."

"You'll miss it, Puff, I tell ye."

Easter Egg Hunting and its Finish.

(*What the Sam Hill.*)

"You boys lay low about this. We don't want everybody to know it."

"You said a while ago you had visited old Bob Wilson; did he know it?"

"Hold on, there! You are insinuating now."

"Well, I was just wondering when——"

"Yes, you are always wondering, and what to wonder at, I'd like to know."

"Well, I'm a little acquainted with him, myself. I was looking for Easter eggs over in that country, and happened near his barn, and he came out and says: 'What you doing out there?'

" 'Looking for some boys.'

" 'You don't happen to find many in that hollow stump, do you?'

"All the time he kept coming closer and nearer, until I thought it about time to be moving, and when I started to run he cut loose, and if that was a sample of his foot-racing I wouldn't wanted to have tackled him in his young days. We clipped along down the slope towards Tom Genn's sugar camp, and I tell ye he gained on me every jump, but when we struck the hill on the other side of the creek, I could hear him puff like Tom Ross' thrashing machine. I knew then I had him. Pretty soon water run low; he had to draw his fire, steam went down, and he called for brakes."

"That was a pretty close call, Puff."

"Yes, but you know we have been in several

[21]

places where we didn't have much wind to spare."

"Yes, that's so; you see I know old Bob, myself. Pa was just talking about him this morning. You see Pa is assessor, and he always has a tussle with old Bob. The other day he slid into Old Bob's feed lot, 'What's that bay hoss worth, Bob?'

" 'Oh, to be honest with ye, he's good for a couple of hundred, I guess; sound in wind and limb, stand hitched anywhere, never been drove to hurt him. Why, are you looking for a hoss?'

" 'No, I'm assessing.'

" 'Great Caesar, is that so?'

" 'Yes, I want to place a valuation on all your stock and different items subject to taxation.'

" 'Oh, well, that's another matter, as I just loud that was what ye was after. Well, that hoss is worth twenty dollars, I reckon.'

" 'You will have to raise that a little, Bob, or the Board will call you out sure.'

" 'What Board?'

" 'Why, the Equalizing Board, of course.'

" 'Pshaw, I'll risk the Board. Don't you worry about the Board. I've lived quite a spell.'

" 'I am not disputing that, but everything goes at full value now, and you know you wouldn't take that. Got any bees?"

[22]

"Dead as a mackeral."

"Any honey in those hives?"

"Reckon not, or they wouldn't died."

On going out to the hives bees were flying in all directions. It was a warm day in January.

"Bob, do you call them dead bees?"

"Well, I'le swan, I was out here the other day and nary a bee in sight. They'll die before spring anyway. I never give in to my bees."

"I'll have to list those at so much a stand, Bob."

"What if they die."

"Well, what if you die; some one must pay the taxes."

"Got any money, Bob?"

"Nary cent."

"Nothing. Under written evidence of credit?"

"Nothing. Nope."

"How's that mortgage on the Kingry place?"

"Well, what about it?"

"Taxable. Written evidence?"

"What! Mortgages?"

"Yes."

"Who pays the taxes on the land."

"The land, of course."

"What, tax the land; then tax the mortgage for the same land. Say, can't ye pile on some

other way to get some more out of it, just as
well. If ye can get two pulls out of it, just
as well have three."

"What other taxable property have you got,
Bob?"

"Well, I guess I'd as well let you fix it. You
seem to know more about it than I do."

"Any gold or silver watches?"

"Nope."

"Got any that's halfway between?"

"What's that?"

"Gold filled."

"There ye go again."

"Yes, what's it worth?'

"Mabe, you know so much."

"What is it; patent leavers?"

"Now ye have hit it. I leaver most every
time I'm in town. Every fellow I take it to
says here, this watch is dirty; it needs clean-
ing. That watch has gathered enough dirt
since I owned it to make a good-sized south
forty."

"How would forty dollars catch it?"

"It would have to do a better job of running
than it ever did for me, if it did not catch it."

"Well, that's about right, isn't it?"

"Why, of course not. I got it in the first
place with tobacco tags, and they are only
worth half cent apiece."

"What does that signify if you gave enough
of them?"

[24]

"It signifies this: I only had two thousand of them, and that was only ten dollars."

"But the watch is a good one, and would sell for cash for forty dollars to-day."

"Air ye cashing any watches to-day?"

"No, but I have no doubt I could find you a buyer."

"Well, let's postpone this assessing business till we find him."

"And that's the way it went all the way through. Old Bob pays tax on about ten thousand, which means he has twenty. He's always going on and talking and acting as though there was a pocket in a shroud, and the resurrection a long ways off. He says, though, that he has the rheumatism so bad these times that he can't walk until he runs around a little."

CHAPTER V.

"Hello, Puff; good morning."

"Hello, Dangit; how air ye?"

"All right. When do you think we'd better pull out, Puff."

"Dick thinks it won't pay."

"You ain't been talking, have ye?"

"Oh! I just mentioned it to Dick, and Wib, and Lush Doughty, and a few of the boys."

"You air a good one. How do you expect to slip off now? Just as well had it announced in church."

"Well, if we can't slip off, we've lived here quite a spell. I guess we could stand it a while longer."

"Why, I've got my spy-glass; and I traded Wib out of that old secret-trigger pistol that kicked out of Will Herrils' hand and hurt his thumb, we are all ready to start as soon as the dark of the moon."

"I haven't thot much about it lately."

"Why?"

"You know old Doc Cruse, of course."

"Yes."

"Well, he was over at Charley's last night making out naturalization papers for a fellow;

[26]

"Shaw, Just as Well Have it Announced in Church.

(*What the Sam Hill.*)

said he could vote in twenty-one years, if he
kept out of the pen."

"Shaw, I think that's a pretty slim show to
make a citizen."

"Well, I think Charley and Nerve had better
let the citizen business alone, they had about
all they could feed anyway."

"It's all in with old Doc K. You see, he's
coroner as well as doctor, and when he has
doctored you until he has used up all your sur-
plus cash and what your furniture would
bring, he then gets a pull out of the coroner
business. He once doctored Jake Beyney, and
thought he had about all of Jake's wealth, and
in making out a perscription had failed to notice that on the other side he had made out a
list of jurors for the coroner. Jake happened
to notice it, and concluded if the perscription
was a forerunner to such a proceeding, he
would not get it filled, and got well without it,
and is to-day the father of five happy children.
You see, Old Doc feels it his duty to follow
a fellow along down close to the valley and
the shadow, and charge him according to the
length of the valley, and then step in at so
much per diam from the county in the way of
coroner's duties.

"No one ever knew when they saw him driv-
ing along the road whether the ferryboat was
on the other side, or so many candles wanted;
but when a close scrutiny was made and numerous persons were seen wending that way,

all doubts were allayed. Blackstone reigned
and not Dr. Chase. He once treated a fellow
for falling off of hair. He had a strong guar-
antee on the hair deal. The patient discov-
ered that Doc run several kinds of business,
and that some of them wouldn't stand the
light, so he slid out one night leaving a line
that he'd like to find a cure for baldness without resorting to the guillotine.

He usually thought it his duty to either
have his hand on a fellow's pulse or in his
pocket, and was usually pretty well posted
as to the state of either.

Old Doc is a firm believer of the sulphurus
waves licking the shores of the valley and
gobbling up the lost in the end. Between you
and me, I'm thinking he will ride some of them
waves himself. I believe if he was a relative
of mine I would gladly concede the fact.

Now, I don't believe in setting the world
afire. I believe in just plodding along in the
even tenor of our ways. If not in our tenor,
we will take the bass or some minor part, and
not figure too much on being foreman of the
grand jury of the next world. None of us
need be so very particular, as we all no doubt
have friends in both places.

I have never aspired to great things, and
would just as soon as not let some one else
find the bills and turn them over to the court
in the final roundup.

We used to think while sitting in the back

[28]

of the courtroom that if we was one of that jury we would make it hard for that fellow, and now as the last jury is about to set on our case, we imagine we have cut our last armload of stove wood and shoveled our last hod of coal.

For we read of another kind of fuel used in the place from 'whence no traveler returns' and to which my Sunday school teacher once told me I was rapidly galloping.

That may be all right, Puff, but I wouldn't care after working hard all summer and soaking my last two months wages in a suit of clothes to fall into Inocuous disuitude and sink to the same depth obtained by M'Ginty.

CHAPTER VI

"How air ye, Lush?"

"Oh, pretty well; feel a little sleepy, is all."

"Up the pike last night?"

"Oh, no."

"Don't yarn, Lush; seen ye going."

"Well, what if I did? Nothing going on in town. What would you have a fellow do?"

"I can remember, Lush, when you thought there was enough going on; that was when you was one of the boys. Forgot it, Lush?"

"No, not particular; but a fellow can't always stick to blackman and hide and ka hoop, from the old hay scales."

"No, but you held your own when you was there."

"Where was you last night, Dangit?"

"I was over at the potter shop kiln."

"What was goin' on?"

"Well, you know Scott Shirk, who tinkers clocks, sometimes?"

"Yes."

"Well, Tom Ross came to see Scott, and asked him to go over to his house and look at his clock.

"Scott went over and looked at it, as Tom said; came back and made out his bill. He

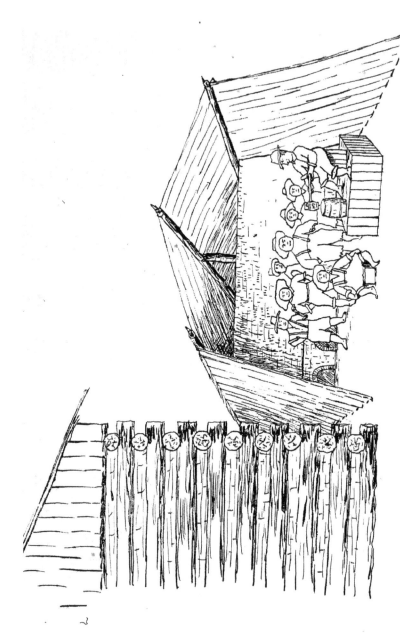

Crackers Neck Court.

(*What the Sam Hill.*)

never touched the clock and never agreed to, but charged for the time going.

"When Tom came home night before last the clock was stopped. He came on to see Scott about it, and had him brought before our Cracker's Neck court. We tried the case that night at the kiln, and we got the decision. You know Wib is judge this term."

"Yes, I would liked to have herd it."

"Well, as I am secretary, it was left with me, so I can send it to you."

"All right."

Important Decision of Cracker's Neck Court.

Whereas, it has become the duty of the incumbent of the Judicial bench in the parish of Cracker's Neck and State of Indiana to decide on the evidence as given in docket 11969, as shown by the records thereof, and the number being indisputable and that fadeth not away.

Whereas, the said Scott Shirk, as plaintiff, and Tom Ross, as defendant,

Be it now understood that the same Scott Shirk, a struggling mechanic of the teutonic art, a mender of watches, clocks, etc., and be it known that on a certain day he was requested to go and look at the calendar clock of Tom Ross,

And be it known that the ancestors of which he is a direct descendant were at one time prominent in fine arts, in fact they can be

[31]

traced along the lagoon of ancient fame. We even find them mentioned as surmounting the peristile of the ancient temple of tyre, dressed in the habilaments of a Chicago actress, wherein the dress consists of a narrow ribbon around the loins, and that left in the check room adjoining the gent's walk where the five-cent turnstyle stares you in the face, and we might here digress and say the greed of man surpatheth understanding, and as I said before, beware of the flowing bowl and of the Crackers Neck docket. Now, as the calling of the said Scott Shirk is an honorable and exhalted one, and as the labor performed by him is a credit to his ancient ancestors, and as the bumps of and a reaching out after lucre is poorly developed and is daily deteriorating, it would behoove the court to a sense of lenency. In his case we find evidence charging him with undue desire for exorbitancy. In fact, it has been proven by a witness of poor but honest parents, that the said Scott Shirk, with malice aforethought, did wilfully and malignantly, as to the said malice, and has been proven and that the funds secured through this instrumentality was in keeping with prices obtained through a person with the blood of his ancestors flowing through his veins, for the "laborer is worthy of his hire," and this is undisputable among workman of this class.

Now, as to the points at issue, of which I have exhaustingly enlarged upon, and as the

character of the aforesaid has been proven
that he is in no wise related to that ancient
animal, the steak and spare ribs of which we
take to with relish regardless of the fact that
the ancestors of which these are direct descen-
dants, and at one time were said to be possess-
ed of the devil, and we should here take heed
and resolve to profit by the teaching of the
docket 11969 and of those brought out in the
evidence, and when the time comes that we
shall sit where he now sits in the culprit's
chair, with the countenance of a Prendegast
and the daring of a Jack Shepherd; that you
can say verily this, a righteous judge and his
court beams on you and of a modern expres-
sion which slops over with benevolence and
lenency. The punishment of this court is that
the said Scott Shirk be debarred from all work
of whatsoever kind, and borrowing of his
neighbors without security, that he be re-
quired to get up at six o'clock in the morning
and sit in the shade while his brothers saw
wood for the day, he shall appear daily in his
usual haunts without being recognized as a
member of the National Federation of Labor,
he shall however be recognized as should a
person with so illustrious a pedigree, and
should his walks of life be such this embryalgo
may be in time lifted from him.

As for Mr. Ross, we have only praise for
one in spite of the combined oratory of the
attorneys of the other side he has manfully

plead his own case. We would however beg
to be relieved from appearing in testimony as
to his truth and varasity. His rebuttal (wherein he states not being able to know the day
of the month from the lack of Mr. Shirk in
performing his work in conformity with his
training), we will look over from the fact that
the constable is supposed to date all papers
before leaving this office. I don't wish to in-
sinuate. He no doubt feels hurt at the treat-
ment received at the hands of the tutonic gen-
tleman, and will feel inclined to stand on the
street corner like the person of old and herald
to the world these facts which have been prov-
en and the ignomineous punishment which
quickly followed the culprit.

We find by looking over the by-laws of the
ancient tyronic metal workers that they merely charged for going to see the work, instead
of for the work done; however, as I made this
discovery after the decision was made, it is too
late to be of benefit to the culprit.

As a higher court will convene here in a few
minutes I would suggest, as some of your
shortcomings are known, that a speedy exit
through the rear door would be advisable.

The janitor will please clear the rear exit as
speedily as possible.

"Pretty good; that sounds a whole lot like
Wib."

"Yes, the boys made it pretty hot for Tom, but he plead his own case and did very well."

"How often does the Crackers Neck meet?"

"Oh, no regular time; mearly when we have a case before it."

CHAPTER VII

Years after.

Puff went back to school, got into a fight with a Jew, and in accordance with the fitness of things came out victorious.

This race of people have been in statu quo for twenty centuries on account of having killed a prominent man without a trial, and aside from Puff having one eye disabled, and his nose crooked in an oblique manner, his wrist put out of place, and his hip knocked down, and a few minor scratches, he escaped unharmed. However, old Wess saw that he was expeled. He worked around awhile at what ever he could get to do, but did not seem to gather much moss.

Dangett worked in a brick yard and spent most of his money in dime novels and got the western fever worse than in his boyhood days.

Wib went northwest and worked in a maple sugar camp awhile, finally drifted to Chicago, and lived in a Sweedish boarding-house, learned to talk the language after a fashion, got mixed up in a strike in which foreigners predominated, came near getting knocked on the head, after the strike was informed that his services were no longer needed, drifted

(*What the Sam Hill.*)

Forty-five Years After.

from one thing to another, got homesick, pawned the first watch he ever owned for half what it was worth, and turned homeward, where he arrived in time to see his old and particular friend on his deathbed.

Six boys carried him to his last resting place out near the old brick school-house, where he rests free from the cares of life. Where are they all this night, fifty years after?

This cast a gloom over the old set. The old loafing corner was never the same again. The old set drifted apart. Some moved away, some married, others died.

And long years passed by. Those who were rich in their youth became poor, and the poor became rich. Old ties were broken.

The remnant of the old set gather to-night around the fire at the old crockery kiln back of the old potter shop. They are now bearded men of two score and ten, some of them more. Quiet prevails. They sit and look into the fire with a sad, wistful look.

"Lyman (Puff of the old boyhood days)," says Tom, "I of all the old set I would rather see Wib than any one in this world."

"Yes, so would I."

"Who's Wib?"

"Oh, you never knew him; he used to live here; left forty years ago, long before you were born."

And Tom, his place was never filled.

You are right, Tom, it took a good one to

[37]

hold him off on "town ball," "bull pen," "old cat," "blackman," foot race or swim.

"Yes, we did not think we would ever be seperated, but see how few of us are left."

"I don't recon he will ever come back here again."

"No, I have not heard from him for years."

"I got a small package from him years ago from old Mexico; he was then away back in the wilds of Mexico, among the cliff dwellings, and wrote me he intended going still farther back in the wilds. We will never see him again, boys, and besides, he is now, like us, getting old. Do you suppose he is any happier than if he had stayed with us?"

"Listen! Some one is coming."

"How do you do, gentlemen?"

"Good evening, sir. Won't you come by the fire? We have plenty of room to-night; but we have seen the time when you would have found it hard to get a place around this fire."

"Thanks, yes; I was just passing through your town and stopped over night. Saw, a light here, and came over."

"You don't live close here?"

"No, I live in the far West."

"Well, you see here around this fire all that is left of a club of boys that have sat here at every burning of this kiln for forty years."

The stranger stood a little in the shadow and looked long and silent into the fire, and finally says, "Is it possible?"

[38]

"Yes, sir, we once numbered ten or twelve careless boys with no thought of the morrow, and, sir, we would give more this night to see the old set here around this fire than to see a whole line of presidents. But they are scattered to the four winds. The meeting will never be. You say you are from the West; you no doubt have traveled much?"

"Yes, indeed, here and there and almost everywhere. I have been from under the flag on the south and on the north. In my youth I suppose I made one of such a club as you describe."

"Here, take this box. I'd just as soon stand up as not."

"Oh, no; keep your seat."

We who have always lived here, it is true have read much and saw pictures of that country, but we would like to hear some of your experience of your travels over it."

"You say you have always lived here? Don't you know you should be the happiest men living? You have stayed because you were contented; and what is money compared with contentment with our lot? You may have missed seeing many grand things, but you are here; have always been here, and now there is no place like this. Wherever a man lives is his allotted place. It is home, no matter where he goes he in time drifts back to it."

"We are not particularly grumbling; we are aware we have had our day."

[39]

"As it is early in the evening, I will give you an outline of one that was not satisfied with his lot. I will begin by saying in my boyhood I was a reader of many sensational novels. I can now see it was a waste of time, but what I got from them caused me to think it the thing to pull out from home. My parents were poor and not particularly in need of me at home. So at rather an early age I severed the home tie and pulled out for the West. I landed in a Western town along in the afternoon, went to a hotel to stay over night. This was not like some of the large hotels you read about, where a boy starts after a glass of water, and is old and gray-headed when he gets back, but one of modest dimentions. I registered with a flourish; told the landlord I was hunting work.

"'Yes, that's all right; I've seen fellows hunting work before. Have you any baggage? For if you have not you will have to pay in advance.'

"'Yes, I've a trunk at the depot.'

"'Here, Jake.'

"'Well, what?'

"'You go down to the depot that has a saloon in the basement with a sign at the head of the stairs,

"'"NOSE PAINT FOR SALE HERE"

and get the trunk this check calls for.'

"'All right.'

[40]

(*What the Sam Hill.*)   The Famous Coril Exchange of Stormy Jourden.

"And from the color of Jake's nose I thought he had been there after baggage before.

"Well, he brought the trunk, placed it in the room, turned the key over to me, and I was the owner pro tem of my first room. I sauntered down into the barroom just as two fellows met. One says, 'Hello, Bill; where been fur a week back?'

"'I haven't got any weak back. What are you talking about?'

"They stormed around in strong conversation relative to their general character, personal appearance, the style of their ancestors, and probable destination when done with this world. It was about as vivid a word picture, and as plain language as I had heard in many a day. I thot it would end in a knockdown, but found it was mearly a mild western way of greeting.

"'Going to the torch light?'

"'Yes, you bet.'

"'All right; let's go out and see how things look.'

"This informed me that there was a torch light in town that night, as the campaign was in full blast. Well, I went out on the street, and being a little chilly, I asked a street vender for a hot lemonade, and the deliberate way he went at it made me think he imagined he was boiling his mother-in-law. He must have been a good one, sure. Yes, I was not used to his

[41]

style, but remembered I was in a strange country, and said nothing.

"The torchlight was grand, the music fine,
and I enjoyed it. One fellow of the opposite
party got hilarious over his favorite candidate,
and in the absence of a man with a trumpet to
herald it to the world, did the herald act himself, and got promptly knocked down and a
lamp stick stuck in his rib. I thought if that
was a sample of the way they did, I would
keep my politics to myself.

"I came back to my room in good time, but
found some one had been there before me. My
trunk was open, my best suit of clothes gone,
and various other things. He had left an in-
ferior pair of pants in their place.

"This floored me completely. I went back
to the barroom.

"'Say, landlord, you was a little particular
about me bringing my trunk here, wasn't you?'

"'Yes, sir, it is our rule.'

"'Well, if you had been as particular about
taking care of it, I would have liked it better.'

"'Why, what's wrong?'

"'Oh, nothing, only some one has gone
through it and about cleaned me out of
clothes.'

"'You don't say so.'

"'Yes, I do; come up to my room.'

"'Well, don't that beat Bob.'

"'I don't know, but I know it beats me out

[42]

of a suit of clothes, and, landlord, I am not feeling very good over it.'

" 'I expect not; we must look into this at once.'

" 'You need not lose any time getting started on my account.'

"We got track of a fellow and followed him from one saloon to another, but when we found him about to board a midnight train with a big grip we stopped him, and had him open it. This he did willingly, but he had nothing of mine. I explained it to him. He says all right, he did not want to leave town under suspicion. I did not find them that night, and have never found them to this day."

"I would call that hard luck to start on."

"Yes, but I got work soon, and got along all right, and stayed there a number of years.

"One day in looking over a scrap of newspaper, I noticed a glowing account of the great strikes in the silver mines of Leadville. Also a description of the trip over the great Union Pacific route from Omaha. The beautiful mountain scenery and Concord coach and I don't know what all. This awakened my restless spirit again, and the desire to see the West again was strong. I decided to go. Quickly making preparations, I started with but little money. On reaching Omaha all was confusion and rush. There was not baggage-cars enough to carry the baggage. We had to go on and leave it to follow. Crossing the plains reminded me of something I had often read about, and was now being realized. The ever-changing landscape was of great interest to us all. Droves of antelope, an occasional coyote, prairie dog towns, miles in length, where thousands of little fat fellows were sitting upright looking at the train go by, just as they looked at the covered wagon go by years before on the Pike's Peak and California trail. We reached Cheyenne, Wyoming. What boy has not read at least one novel where Cheyenne is mentioned? This, beyond North Platte, where the two Platte rivers come together and a Western story with the Platte River left out would be a tame affair, indeed. At Cheyenne we rest for two hours, when we change cars for Denver. This modern city, away beyond the line of civilization, is still a city in every particular. Hotels of every kind, with plenty of sharks to catch the unwary tenderfoot.

"Here we stop one day before taking the narrow guage railway for the mountains. We start the next morning after sizing up the small pony engine at the head of the train and wondering how it will ever pull us up the mountain. No pen or description can do justice to the grandeur displayed while passing through the Platte Canyon. Mile after mile of rock so high that you can hardly see the top; great boulders that look just ready to

leave their bed of centuries and roll down
to our destruction; jets of rock that reach
out almost to the car windows, while the
Platte River that runs so sluggish across the
plains here goes roaring and plunging over
numerous boulders with terrible speed. It
looked as though nothing could keep us from
pitching from the track as we rounded the
sharp curves.

"We are enjoying the magnificent scenery
when we slowly pull into a small mountain
station.

"'Webster!' shouts a train man. 'Change
here for Concord coach!'

"We all scramble out. Here is pande-
monium personified. Great trains of freight
wagons, three coupled together and pulled by
sixteen mules, driven by what was intended
in the start to be one man, but by the way he
cussed and tore around and whipped those
mules you would have thought there was a
dozen.

"We look around and wonder if that old
rickety vehicle is a Concord coach, and if it is
going to Leadville, and are highly enlightened
when we ask some fellow and he tells you 'Go
to ——.'

"We call on the baggageman and present
our checks to have our baggage rechecked to
Leadville, as the party who run the great
Union Pacific ticket office told us 'Oh, yes,
check you right through to Leadville.'

"He tells us it has not arrived yet, and when it does it will not be checked to Leadville. He also tells us it will be forwarded for five dollars per hundred. We now wish we had not crowded in enough to just clear the one hundred and fifty pounds they told us they would allow us. We remonstrated at this, but are shut off in language that satisfies us that the man, although away back in the dim past may have been a Sunday school scholar, he had long since forgotten it. We are informed that checks don't go over a mountain toll road where it costs twenty cents a mile to travel in a coach.

"All things have an end, and so did our jangling; it ended by us retreating and leaving him a clear field, thoroughly satisfied in our minds if he did not get his just dues in this world he would in the next; we got our coach tickets booked, gather up our grips ready to board the first coach that pulls up, and are finally off after praising its beauty and probable comfort, as it is to be our house for the next two days and nights. There was three coach-loads of us. Nine passengers to the coach, and a more motley crew you could not imagine. Many of them had left other places by request, others had left without settling their bill, some few, like myself, were going to try and better their condition, but the most of them were going simply to get away from somewhere.

[46]

"There was one tall, meek-looking fellow that we sized up as a preacher, he seemed so quiet and meek, but the old saying that 'still water runs deep' was personified in his case. He was one kind of man in day time, and another after night.

"I think I never saw his match. While traveling up the mountains we came across a freight wagon off the track, as they called it, and as there was no other road we had to wait for it to get the road clear. You see, the lower side of the road, as it winds around the mountains, is built up with flat stones to hold the grade. This freighter's rear wagon had slewed around a little, and the rear wheel had dropped over the wall. This completely stalled the whole outfit, and the accident happened on such a sharp curve that the entire sixteen mules could not pull at it. The leaders would, in straightening out the chain, pull the middle teams over against the bank on the upper side of the road. Some of our crowd got out to help clear the wreck, and one fellow that knew it all, back in Virginia, undertook to tell the teamster how to drive. The quiet man stepped up to stop him from interfering, but was too late. The teamster looked at him a moment, then the sulphureous waves began to roll up, and came crashing along, and the under toe completely swept him off his feet. He floundered in the depths but a moment, then figuratively disappeared

[47]

from sight. I think I have heard swearing in all of its purity and clearness, but never heard a man get such a raking fore and aft.

"In time we all got out, and as the night was chilly and snow was falling, we made up a log heap and set fire to it and stayed there until near midnight. Around this fire is where our quiet friend came out in his true colors, and by the time the freight team got out of the way he had most of the money in the crowd. I myself fought shy of him, as I did not like his looks.

"At midnight we loaded into the coaches and pulled out for Fairplay, which we reached some time in the night.

"Promptly at eight o'clock the next morning the coaches were ready to start with fresh teams. Wall and Whittier did not let any grass grow on a toll road. They were the Ben Halidays of the mountains of that date.

"We got along on the second day singing songs and enjoying ourselves as well as we could in our cramped quarters, when:

" 'Here, you fellows will have to walk up this hill.'

"Here was a go. Twenty cents a mile and walk. We all pile out to walk up this hill, which proves to be eight miles long, and almost as steep as a house roof. We could outtravel the coaches, and at the first station where they changed teams we went on ahead and did not see them for half a day.

"The road was more rough and steep as we neared the top of the pass, and the snow more heavy. The wind blew a hurricane. We were so far ahead of the coach we feared had broken down and we would be elected to spend the night in the mountains. We set down behind a tree with our backs to the storm and the snow came trinkling down our backs. The flaming Union Pacific poster came before our eyes describing the beautiful Concord coach and the magnificent mountain scenery on this glorious trip to Leadville.

"We decide to wait near the summit for the coach to come up. When it came up, it proved to be a common lumber wagon, with all our grips piled primiscuous over the bottom of the bed. We all pile in, when: 'Hell! here, you, git off my valice; yiu'v busted it.' We all look, and sure enough and there protruding through the aperture is the leg of the old family rooster who has crowed for the last time and is now accompanying his master on this glorious trip to Leadville.

"As we cross the summit the high air affected one fellow so that over he went. We were all frightened at this, but there was nothing to it but lay him in on the pile of grips and trust to his coming to when we got lower down the mountain. The driver told us it was nothing uncommon. Just then another fellow says: 'Boys, I'm as sick as a horse.'

"'York,' says another fellow, as he leans

[49]

over the side of the wagon and wonders at the
tenacity ·of his boots in staying in place. 'it
took the cake for all the glorious trips I ever
experienced, and really now I would not have
called it that if the U. P. poster had not filled
us up so with the glorious part of it.'

"After getting several thousand feet lower
down our sick man revived just as the driver
told us he would. We shake the snow off our
backs and begin again to enjoy life.

"At a station down toward the park we
again find a coach and roll along in fine shape.
At ten o'clock at night the second night out
we pull into Leadville, a city that at that date
could well be called one of the wonders of the
world.

"Here was man from every corner of the
earth, thousands of them. Many of them
landed without a dollar. No blankets, nowhere
to sleep, every lodging house crowded to its
utmost. Bunk houses, where the bunks were
but little over one foot apart, and one above
another, clear to the top. Greek and Moslem,
Jew and Gentile, Yankee from the Nutmeg
country to cross swords with the mine-salter
of the West. A conglomeration of human be-
ings never before equaled and never will be
again. There was said to be sixty thousand
men on the streets of Leadville and probably
three hundred women, and in all of this mass
not a single family in the city. Tongue nor
pen can never describe it; possession was nine

points of law, and violation caused pistol practice that would beat our old-time Christmas carnivals."

"Well, stranger, that was certainly an interesting time, or trip."

"Yes, and it makes me want to get out there, as old as I am. You know I always wanted to go, Lime?"

"Yes, and I have often wondered why you didn't."

"I never had that much money at one time."

"You are just as well off, my friend."

"Yes, a fellow hates to think of always living in some hole of a place, and in the end finish up by stepping from one hole into another."

"Stranger, you have interested us very much, but it is not late, and we would like to know something of the customs of the country; how are claims obtained? What is the title? We read of jumping claims. How can one man take another's claim? Does not the government protect the title?"

"The customs of the country are based somewhat on law and some on local arrangement. For instance, a mining camp or district taking in a certain bounded territory will arrange in that district to stand by certain rules adopted at a meeting of all claim-holders in that district. All grievances are brought before a certain committee. An appeal can be taken to the courts of the State, or United States, but an

[51]

agreement entered into at the time of organizing is that they will abide by certain rules. The government requires you to set stakes at the corners of your claim and also a location stake on which you state your claim so many feet each way from this stake. The different counties regulate the sizes of claims in that county. The government requires you to do at least $100 worth of work each year, called assessment work, and file with the county recorder a sworn statement that such work has been done. The local district organization requirements may be that you must find mineral before locating or recording your claim. This shows why some jump claims. They say you have no mineral. I will also prospect here, and if I find mineral first, I claim the right to run my claim in any direction I choose.

"That is what causes trouble. The party finding mineral first usually surveys in all the adjoining shafts he can."

"I can now see where the trouble comes in. When a man has worked hard all season he does not like to have his work appropriated by another."

"That is the idea, exactly. Now as to finding or starting a new district and the hardships encountered I will give you a description of a trip I was in which will give you an idea of that part of it. There was a party of three of us started from Leadville to go a distance of eighteen miles over a low pass in the mountains to locate some property. The crust on the snow, which was very deep, would still hold the weight of a man, but it was getting late in the winter and the crust was liable to break through before long. We provided against this by taking some boards ten inches wide by four feet long to strap on our feet in case it did break through. As we expected to get up to the place and get through and back to the trail the same day, we did not take much grub along.

"We got near the place the first day and went into camp, and started early the next morning up the mountains. We got along fine. The place we wanted to get to was one and a quarter miles from the trail. Keep that part in your mind. We got there, staked out our claims and started back. The sun, in the meantime, had come out quite warm and I hurried the other fellows to get back to the trail.

"This trip was made after I had spent one season in the mountains, while the other fellows were tenderfeet. We had not gone far down the mountain before the crust began to break through. We would sink into the snow over our heads, flounder awhile and get up on top again. The crust would again break, our shoes would turn over on edge, and in all kinds of shapes, while into the deep snow we would go again. You who have almost gave out wading in snow hip deep can have a little idea

[53]

of the way it would be over your head—you
simply can't make headway. The snow soon
became very wet and we were soon wet to the
skin. We would button our overcoats tight
up around us, roll our blankets (something you
dare not leave behind, as the nights are cold),
around us and try to roll down the mountain.
This would do for a short distance but in time
we gradually sank beneath the surface again.
I soon saw we were in a dangerous predica-
ment. The others did not realize the danger,
not being used to the country. We worried
along until noon, then stopped for dinner. The
others were for eating everything to avoid
carrying it, but this I would not allow, as I
knew we were elected for a night in the mountains. After dinner we started again, working
with indifferent success. Night came on. We
took our snow shoes and shoveled away until
we reached the ground. Here we made a fire.
Our matches we carried in waterproof boxes.
We made our coffee and eat our last bite of
grub. We then set some forks in the snow at the
edge of our dugout, laid a pole across and
broke pine boughs off the trees nearby, and
made a bed, we also covered the roof of the
dugout with them. This made quite a snug
little shanty. As dead brush was plenty we
provided quite a supply of it for the fire. Then
pulled the roof covering in place over our
heads and prepared to spend the night. The
other two were inclined to make light of it,

but I knew we were in a tight place. Along some time before spreading our blankets on the pine boughs, one of the boys had thrown a piece of ham bone on the fire. This burnt and sputtered quite awhile, and made quite a smoke, but it worked out through the roof and did not bother us.

"It commenced to snow very hard in the night, as it often does in that latitude in March and April. A light fluffy snow. We had laid down in our wet clothes and wet blankets, all snug up together, and got up quite a steam from the heat of our bodies, and once in a while some fellow would snore a few whiffs, but not long at a time, as our uncomfortable position would soon wake him up.

"Along some time in the night, we supposed from the smell of the burnt bone, a mountain lion had scented it, and came along to find it, and came right up to the brink of our dugout, and I suppose smelling us, raised the worst howl or screech I ever heard. The tenderfoot sleeping in the middle jumped to an upright position at one jump and hollered: 'What the hell's that!' struck his head against the ridge pole, knocked it out of the fork and down came our roof with six inches of snow right among our blankets. This was grand in the extreme, and no one seemed at a loss for language to express himself, in fact the time seemed ripe for all hands to express themselves without leave from the chair. Roberts' Rules of Order were

[55]

shelved for a time, and bedlam but a short ways off. It would be hard to say which was frightened the worst, the lion or the tenderfoot. The lion made off at a lively rate.

"This ended the sleeping for that night. It took quite a while to quiet the fellow and convince him that we were in no particular danger' from the lion."

" 'Well, you get us out of this scrape and you can have all the claims. I, myself, am out of it.

"We sat down and hugged our knees until morning and a more dilapidated set you never saw.

"We started out without any breakfast, and I was sure we would not get any dinner, as we were still three-fourths of a mile from the trail. We rolled and pitched and tried all kinds of ways, but made but slow progress. Noon came and no dinner. I, myself, was getting very weak. Now near two days in the wet snow and but little to eat in that time. I could hardly stand on my snow shoes when I got them placed on top of the snow. Along about two o'clock in the afternoon one of the tenderfeet rolled over in the snow and says: 'Here you fellows, just go; I'm all in; plum played. I'll never move another peg, it's no use, boys; I've been watching, Wib, and I tell ye we can never make it, and I won't try any more.'

"This was serious indeed, as I knew to leave him meant death. We were all about played

[56]

as far as that was concerned, but I knew we must reach the trail that night or we would never reach it. I pictured to him that there was a shanty about a mile down the trail from where we would strike it, and if we only could make it we would get plenty to eat and a place to sleep. We worked and reasoned with him for a long time, and after loosing a lot of valuable time he got up and started. We were in plain sight of the trail and must reach it. Night came on and with it a snow storm. We still were several rods from the trail. The tenderfeet were in for going into camp, but I knew better than to try to stem another night in our weak state, so urged them to renewed exertion, telling them we were so close to the trail and safety that we must reach it, and reach it we did, and when my feet struck the solid trail it seemed to me I could win a foot race with any one.

"We rolled up our blankets. I took the lead, calling for them to follow, as I knew the trail. We pulled into the shanty about midnight, the third night out. The miners got up and made us some strong tea. I was setting on the side of the bunk at the time, and that was the last I knew until some time the next morning; he said I drank a tin cup of hot tea and dropped over backwards on the bunk, and was sound asleep and never moved the whole night. He stayed up the remainder of the night to keep up a hot fire as we were still in our wet

[57]

clothes. The dinner they gave us has never been equaled by Delmonico. It put life into us and soon after we pulled out for Leadville.

"One of the fellows stayed around our shanty a few days, but came in one morning and said: 'Good-bye, boys, I've got enough of this. The stage starts in half an hour,' and in spite of all we could say he bid us good-bye. As he wrung my hand he says, 'Wib, I'll tell the folks that it was you that saved my life on that awful trip. I'm not built for this country, farewell,' and that was the last time I ever saw him. He went back into the States, took down with rheumatism, and the last I heard of him he was a physical wreck.

"The other fellow stayed around the most of the summer, but I could never get him to go near the claims, and in the fall he disappeared, and that is the last I ever saw of him. The claims proved worthless and so ended the most perilous trip of my life."

"Um, hum'. Lime, what do ye think of that? Want any mountains in yours?"

"Not by a long chalk, but I would not have missed hearing about it for any thing. We are certainly obliged to you, stranger, for your story."

During this time, Tom (the Danget of boyhood days), is eyeing the stranger. Several times during the recital the tone of his voice, some particular motion or twist called up old memories. A slight scar across the forehead, another across the first fingers of the right hand was quite plain, and the conviction somes crowding on him all at once. This is your old chum, Wib.

"Boys, the story is ended. I couldn't stay away any longer. I am Wib."

"Great Caesar, don't that beat you."

"It's no use talking I ought to have known you sooner, but forty years is a long time, and you are changed. Well, I should say so. But an old-time whoop, I've no doubt will bridge the chasm and bring you back to us again."

"Come over to the store and see if any of the men will know you, Tom. This is the best night I ever saw. Gee, how I wish all the old set was here to-night."

"That's what's the matter."

"Over at the store. Forty years to span. Who is here? Who has fallen by the wayside? When the roll is called who will answer?"

Lime is spokesman.

"Gentlemen, what do you think we have found to-night over at the old potter shop kiln. One who bade us good-bye forty years ago. He steps into his old corner and entertains us for hours with his travels, but by watching close and listening to his voice or seeing some particular move or tone we figure him out. This, gentlemen, is our old-time Wib, after forty years wanderings returns to us."

"What's that you are saying, Lime? Wib. You can't fool me on Wib. I was along when

[59]

he was accidentally struck with a rock on the forehead. I would know that scar any where."

"Yes, and I was there when he got the two first fingers of his right hand sawed on Tom Genn's lathe saw."

"All right, here is your scars, and let me tell you who you are: Your are John Duket, you Dave Genn, Bill Willson. How are you Henry Harvey, glad to see you. Scott Pettygrew, you are the same old Scott, and this is John Webb. Tom Trusler, are you still with Jake Masters? Tom Powers, when I get a good look into them eyes, I knew you. Is that you Kinard? Glad to see you. Dave, if there was a sap suck out here on that locust tree I would show him to you."

THE END.

OUR NEWEST ISSUES

By James A. Ritchey, Ph.D.
Psychology of the Will.....................$1.50

By Charles Hallock, M. A.
Peerless Alaska 1.00

By Dwight Edwards Marvin.
Prof. Slagg of London..................... 1.50
The Christman 1.50

By Caroline Mays Brevard.
Literature of the South.................... 1.50

By Susan Archer Weiss.
Home Life of Poe (3d ed.).................. 1.50

By Irving Wilson Voorhees, M.D.
Teachings of Thomas Henry Huxley (2d ed.). 1.00

By Mrs. Annie Riley Hale.
Rooseveltian Fact and Fable............... 1.00

By Hon. D. W. Higgins.
The Mystic Spring......................... 1.50

By Edith Nicholl Ellison.
The Burnt-Offering 1.25

OUR NEWEST ISSUES

By Alexandre Erixon.
The Vale of Shadows........................ 1.50

By Mrs. Josephine M. Clarke.
The King Squirrel of Central Park (Juvenile). .60

By William N. Freeman.
St. Mammon 1.50

By Mrs. I. Lowenberg.
The Irresistible Current.................... 1.50

By M. Y. T. H. Myth.
Tales of Enchantment...................... 1.00
A Tale Confided by the Woods.............. .75

By Ida Blanche Wall.
Comedy of Petty Conflicts.................. 1.25

By Elizabeth Helene Freston.
Poems (portrait) beautifully bound.......... 1.00
Italia's Fornarina (leather)................. 3.00

Compiled by Darwin W. Esmond.
Poetry of Childhood, by Paul Warner Esmond
(Memorial Edition) 1.50

OUR NEWEST ISSUES

By Wilbert C. Blakeman.
The Black Hand............................ 1.50

By John W. Bennett.
Roosevelt and the Republic................... 1.50

By Hon. Joseph M. Brown.
(Governor of Georgia.)
Astyanax—An Epic Romance............... 1.50

By John Tracy Mygatt.
What I Do Not Know of Farming............ .75

By Esmee Walton.
Aurora of Poverty Hill...................... 1.50

By Josephine Merwin Cook.
Bandana Days .... .75

By Howard James.
The Wraith of Knopf and Other Stories....... 1.00

By George Fuller Golden.
My Lady Vaudeville and Her White Rats..... 2.00

By J. A. Salmon-Maclean.
Leisure Moments 1.00
A Stricken City............................ .50

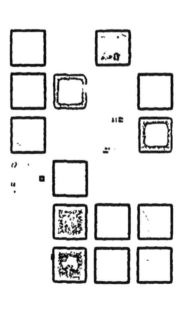

Lightning Source UK Ltd.
Milton Keynes UK
UKHW020637250321
380972UK00005B/318